What to Say to Your
CRAZY RIGHT–WING UNCLE
Talking Points for Liberals

By
Samuel Warren Joseph
&
Phil Proctor

Foreword By Thom Hartmann

Sam/Phil Books

Print ISBN: 978-0-57861-448-9
Ebook ISBN: 978-0-57861-497-7
Printed in the United States
Cover design and book layout by Brett Davidson
Illustrations by Phil Fountain

Foreword:

Former Australian Prime Minister Kevin Rudd recently wrote an op-ed for the Sydney Morning Herald titled "Cancer Eating the Heart of Australian Democracy." In it, Prime Minister Rudd says that Rupert Murdoch is "the greatest cancer on the Australian democracy." He notes how Murdoch, even today, manipulates and controls politicians through his media dominance in Oz – he "owns two-thirds of the country's print media."

Rudd then points out that Murdoch took his poison to Great Britain, where he helped engineer a rightwing takeover of British politics through much the same strategy, and then moved on to the US, where he started Fox so-called News, which is today poisoning American political discourse.

How did we get here?

In 1976, the US Supreme Court, for the first time in the history of our nation, declared that when a billionaire wants to buy and own a politician, that's no longer considered bribery or corruption – the cash itself being spent by that billionaire is now constitutionally-protected First Amendment "free speech," and can't meaningfully be regulated by the government. The Buckley v Valeo decision blew up a century of good-government laws regulating money in politics.

It was followed two years later with the 1978 First National Bank v Bellotti decision, which extended the logic to corporations. (It was also the Supreme Court that decided – against the will of a century of Congress and over the objections of presidents past and present – that corporations were actually "persons" entitled to "human rights" under the Bill of Rights and the 14th Amendment.)

i

The Supreme Court opened the door to control of the American media and political scene, and the billionaire and corporate class walked right in and took over. A small ocean of money followed the First National Bank decision in 1979 and 1980, bringing Ronald Reagan to power and setting up decades of Republican rule.

That led right to Bill Clinton, politically indebted to a group of banking, insurance and media billionaires, to sign the Telecommunications Act of 1996, which blew up FCC rules that limited the number of newspapers, radio and TV stations that an individual billionaire or his corporation could own.

It's not just one man and his business, of course, who have so coarsened our politics – there are other billionaires, like when Mitt Romney's company engineered a takeover of Clear Channel and began dumping Air America's progressive programming from station after station, eventually helping put that progressive network out of business.

Or the billionaire Dickey brothers who bought around 500 radio stations via their company, Cumulus, along with buying Westwood One, the last syndicator of progressive content in the United States…that now no longer syndicates progressive content. And the Smith family that controls Sinclair Broadcast Group, with their regular rightwing rants pushed down to hundreds of local TV stations. Or the conservative Roberts family that built Comcast.

Additionally, there are dozens of smaller and more local or regional players, all devoted to the idea that corporations and rich people should run things, democracy be damned.

The consequence of all this is that much of our media has been turned into an incessant rightwing propaganda machine, with Fox News and a handful of multimillionaire talk radio hosts setting its direction and pace.

And the consequence of that is a lot of confused uncles.

In "What to Say," Sam and Phil provide both a template for talking back to your Crazy Uncle (who's not really crazy, just misinformed) and a narrative script, both as example and detail. It's a small but important step in reclaiming truth and sanity in the midst of an insane and often nakedly untruthful media landscape.

Read this book, share it, memorize it, and, most important, use it.

If we're to stop the growth of neoliberalism and open Nazism here in the United States, we all must speak out.

Organized people can defeat organized money – it just takes a lot of time and effort. But movement after movement, from the founding of America, have proven it possible. So, using the incredible tool of this book, get out there and get active.

Tag, you're it!

Thom Hartmann

Preface:

I first knew of Phil Proctor and the amazing comic quartet he was a part of, Firesign Theatre, when I was in college. Years later, we met at the Writers' Guild but I truly got to know Phil in 2006 when he agreed to be in my play, "Window of Opportunity", a dark comedy about corporate corruption, and later when he co-starred in the film version I directed. That project was very much about slimy business types like Enron's Jeffrey Skilling and Ken Lay and their political allies in the Bush Administration. We so enjoyed working together on that project that we decided to find other projects to collaborate on – one of which is "God Help Us", a political comedy starring Ed Asner that is currently playing around the country. If you are sensing a theme here, you would be right. Phil and I are both political junkies, very well informed, and both believe strongly in progressive values and a vibrant democracy. Seeing what has been going on politically for far too long, and particularly the last few years, inspired us to write this book.

We want to thank Phil's beautiful wife, Melinda Peterson, and my beautiful wife, Sandra Darnel: and in no particular order Ed Asner, F.X. Feeney, Allison Barenbrug, Barry Lynn, John Densmore, Tom Bourgeois, Dr. Beverly Goode-Kanawati, Nabil Kanawati, Gypsy Hartman, Dave Pallack, Brett Davidson, Betsey Brubaker, Phil Fountain, Jamie Alcroft, Bill Ratner, Chandler Warren, Dan Castellaneta, Roy Zimmerman, John Goodman, and Thom Hartmann for writing the Foreword; and all the contributors over the years to PlanetProctor.com.

Introduction:

We live in strange times. We have a grossly corrupt con artist and reality show host in the White House, elevated to this great office despite his lies and manifest incompetence. Millions of people have been brainwashed by a drumbeat of falsehoods and exaggerations that have polluted the public discourse for the past four decades. It is like we are in a car with a drunk driver and are just praying we get home in one piece.

The great difficulty in arguing with those who support this state of affairs is not that there is any simple difference of opinion. There is not even an agreement on simple facts. People -- often, our loved ones -- will chronically assert things that are simply untrue. Certain things have been repeated so many thousands of times that many fall into the trap of believing these must be true, despite the lessons of history. "Tell a lie often enough," preached Hitler's media man, Joseph Goebbels, "and it becomes the truth." We know where that led.

Believers of any great lie will gaslight, deflect, deny. Our aim is to lead the fight in counteracting such deception through logic and reasoned arguments. We uphold the use of reliable, agreed-upon facts. That is why we wrote this book.

Anyway -- that is what my co-author says, but we are no longer speaking.

TALKING POINTS

Chapter One:
LIAR-IN-CHIEF

YOUR RIGHT–WING UNCLE SAYS:

Okay, nephew, you said you wanted to talk to me about something. What's on your mind?

The same thing that is on everybody's mind, Uncle. Donald Trump.

I'm proud to talk about him. Donald Trump says it like it is and that's why you liberals hate him.

I don't hate him, Uncle. And I know you like that Trump is willing to go after his opponents. But the problem is that he lies more than any other President. He averages 13 lies a day. Heck! As of today, PolitiFact has already counted over 14,000 lies. And that's not counting all the lies he told while he was running for President.

Do you remember some of those?

He claimed that Obama's birth certificate was phony without any proof.

He said that he wasn't trying to do a business deal with Russia, while he was talking to them about a Moscow Trump Tower. Remember?

According to the Mueller Report there were 272 contacts with the Russians while Trump claimed that nobody in his campaign had anything to do with them! And he lied about the Trump Tower meeting between Don Jr., his son-in-law, Jared Kushner, and Trump's campaign manager, Paul Manafort.

And the lies he told as President include, well, just about everything!

Believe it or not, Uncle, records show that Trump lies over 60% of the time! But who's counting?

What are you getting so upset about? All politicians lie.

Perhaps, but not all lies are the same.

Didn't Obama say you could keep your doctor?

A perfect example of false equivalency. In fact, most people could keep their doctors on Obamacare, and he was making an argument for a program that helps people get and keep their healthcare.

He was still lying.

Even if he said something that wasn't true, it was still unintentional and not comparable to the stuff Trump makes up all the time – filling people with fear in order to cover up his illegal activities. He tells so many lies so often, people throw up their hands because they don't know what's real and what isn't anymore. As Kellyanne Conway says, believe our "Alternative Facts," which are lies.

A fact is a fact. It is not a falsehood.

It is if the facts are false! Either something is true or it is not.

In your opinion.

And that's the problem right there. People will only believe facts that they want to believe – or as Paul Simon sang, "A man hears what he wants to hear and disregards the rest."

I wouldn't know. I'm a country music fan.

The point is that sometimes when politicians lie it is relatively harmless or they're trying to better the world by persuading people of something positive. But more often I'm afraid they're trying to fool people to pass laws that actually hurt them – like the tax cut for the rich. But nobody lies as much as Trump. And that's the truth!

Chapter Two:

KIDS IN CAGES

Wait a minute. You can't deny that the invasion of illegal immigrants from Mexico has flooded the country with rapists and drug dealers, just like Donald Trump says.

Not really, Uncle.

Oh, yeah? Prove it.

Well, believe it or not, American citizens actually commit more crimes. For instance, three-quarters of all drug traffickers are U.S. citizens and most of the drugs are smuggled through legal ports of entry - as are guns, too, by the way. And as for sexual assaults, I'm sorry to say, we Americans commit more than immigrants do, legal or illegal.

Well, even if that's so – you can't deny that illegal immigrants are taking all our jobs.

Well, if you want to pick strawberries all day, Uncle, I'll ask José if you can take his place. Do you want your daughter to give up her nanny, her gardener and her house cleaner?

What I'm trying to say is that illegal immigrants are doing jobs that most Americans won't.

Look, immigrants are the backbone of our nation. And I know that my Dad and yours came from Europe, and we even have a Cajun cousin in New Orleans.

Yeah, but we're legal. We're citizens.

However, your ancestors weren't at first, but eventually they earned their citizenship.

But look at the caravans and hordes of people trying to come here now. What are you going to do about that?

Well, first off, I wouldn't put kids in cages. Are you happy we're doing that Uncle? I know you better than that.

If these immigrants don't want to be separated from their kids, they shouldn't have brought them in the first place.

They're desperate. Most of the folks trying to come here are terrified people escaping from violence and poverty in Central America. We should be doing something to fix that and not punishing these desperate refugees.

And the truth is while immigration rates have been going up and down for decades, the overall number of immigrants remains about the same in relationship to our population. And in general, studies show that illegal border crossings have declined!

And we're going to stop them completely when Trump finishes building his beautiful wall.

You mean the one that Mexico was going to pay for and Congress refused to fund?

Yeah, that do-nothing Congress. That's why he had to declare a National Emergency to get the money.

By taking it away from military families and programs that keep them healthy and educated. That only makes us weaker. As a veteran, do you like that, Uncle?

He's just doing what has to be done to protect us.

But it won't protect us, and it won't keep people out. Most people here illegally just overstayed their visas. They didn't sneak in. A wall is a waste of money.

Chapter Three:
WHITE ON WHITE

Okay. Maybe some of things you're saying are true. But you have to admit, white people like us are under attack.

What is under attack, Uncle, is the American ideal of diversity, where all sorts of people are living together. Trump is trying to scare white people with the propaganda of paranoia by telling us how dangerous minorities are.

And what is the result? A rise in white nationalism – The Proud Boys – modern day Brown Shirts – you know, the NAZIS: the fascists grandpa fought against in World War II.

Those people are just overreacting because of all the advantages minorities are getting. Look at Affirmative Action.

The reason we have that is because of all the years minorities were discriminated against. I do think that as society gets more color blind, the less we'll need it.

And I suppose you want to pay African-Americans reparations for what happened all those years ago.

I have mixed feelings about that idea, Uncle. There still is a lot of discrimination, particularly in the justice system that we need to address. The most important change I would like to see is minorities less harassed by the police.

Chapter Four:
THE COMMIES ARE COMING

You have to admit that race is still a big problem in our country.

Well, I'm not a racist, but I am a realist, and it is obvious that most welfare is for minority freeloaders. We pay taxes to support those welfare cheats.

Well, guess what Uncle - most of the people on welfare, who get food stamps, are older...like you! And they pay taxes, like you! And most of them are white! Like you!

Yeah, but I'm not on welfare.

Yes, and we can all agree that there are too many people - of all colors - on welfare. And why? Because people are working full time at Walmart and still need Medicaid and food stamps to survive. The problem is lack of fair wages and income inequality. The top 1% own 40% of all the wealth in the U.S.A.

They earned that money!

Some did, and some were just members of the 'lucky sperm club,' like your favorite President.

What's obscene is how much more the CEOs of giant corporations make compared to their average employee - sometimes three to four hundred times more! Look at Mary Barra, the CEO of General Motors who made around 22 million bucks last year, 218 times the salary of the average worker.

It's a rigged game.

So what do you want to do smart guy, replace it with socialism?

You mean like Medicare, which paid for your surgery? Or the Post Office, that delivers your mail? Or the military that defends us? The police and fire departments and public schools? The

Library where you read your "Guns & Ammo" magazine? Our capitalism is mixed with socialism. Sometimes we need to act as a group, and sometimes as an individual. And in a democracy we are always working to find the balance.

You're really mixed up. Obamacare is pure socialism and should be abolished.

Are you trying to make me sick, Uncle? Just kidding. Obamacare primarily regulates the _private health insurance industry_ because too many people couldn't afford policies or were prevented from getting one because of pre-existing conditions, like your diabetes. And the public part, or socialism - if you want to call it that - was designed to expand Medicaid for the really poor among us.

Okay, so maybe Obamacare isn't pure socialism, but 'Medicare for all' is. In fact, it's communism!

Come on, Uncle. Great Britain has universal health care, which is the same as Medicare for all. So does Canada, Norway, Denmark, France, Italy, Israel, Germany, New Zealand, Hong Kong and Japan and on and on! Thirty-two countries in all...and none of them are communist, and by the way, health care in Putin's Russia is nyet good.

Chapter Five:
COLLUSION CONFUSION

SPEAKING FOR MYSELF, THERE WAS **NYET** COLLUSION!

I'm glad you brought up Russia because now, according to the Mueller Report, we know for sure there was absolutely no collusion between the Trump campaign and the Russians. It's a collusion delusion.

Oh, Uncle. Where should I start? Mueller never said anything about collusion. He just didn't think he had enough evidence for a criminal conspiracy. But there was plenty of collusion. Don

Jr.'s meeting with the Russians in Trump Tower to get dirt on Hillary. Trump asking the Russians to hack into her emails...which they did! Then they passed the info to WikiLeaks, which was coordinating with the Trump Campaign. And his campaign manager, Paul Manafort, who is now in jail, was giving the Russians polling data. It's pretty clear the Russkies used the data to help Trump on Facebook by spreading disinformation and divisiveness.

C'mon! The Mueller Report exonerated President Trump, and you know it!

I know what Mueller said and that is he COULD NOT exonerate the President, and all but said that he obstructed justice. It's clear that if he were not the President, he would be indicted.

You lefties are using every trick in the book to paint this President as illegitimate. It's all fake news and it's not going to work.

And I suppose his talking to the Russians about building a Trump Tower in Moscow was all fake news?

He's a businessman. What's wrong with that? He wasn't even President then.

That's true. But during the whole campaign Trump swore that he had nothing to do with any Russians in any way, while in fact his campaign had almost 300 documented contacts with Putin's people.

He's trying to get along better with Russia. That's good foreign policy.

It's about as good as giving the green light to Turkey to annihilate our allies, the Kurds, who fought against ISIS with us. Most all of the Republicans in the Congress are furious at this betrayal.

The Commander in Chief, in his 'great and unmatched wisdom', knows what he's doing – even if we don't.

So he can do no wrong? Do you really think his "perfect phone call" with the President of Ukraine wasn't a masked threat to get information to smear Joe Biden and his son?

Yeah, I'm glad you brought up all this impeachment crap. It's a coup, plain and simple. Read the transcript! It's just an attempt to negate the majority who voted for Trump.

The majority actually voted for Hillary, remember? Three million more votes.

Well, he was still elected, and if the liberals are unhappy, they should just wait for the next election, which he's gonna win.

The Congress has a duty to keep a President in check, especially one who is violating his oath of office, making money from other countries, obstructing justice, and betraying our allies like the Europeans and the Kurds while undermining NATO.

Chapter Six

WHICH WITCH IS WHICH?

THE DEEP STATE, THE FBI,
THE CIA, THE NSA, CONGRESS,
AND THE AMERICAN PEOPLE
ARE ALL OUT TO GET ME!
AND DON'T CALL ME PARANOID!

And what about that phony Steele Dossier? The truth is that it was Crooked Hillary who was working with the Russians, not Trump.

The former FBI Director said emphatically that Putin hated Hillary so much he was working behind the scenes to help Trump get elected. Putin even said he wanted Trump to win at their summit in Helsinki. All the intelligence agencies have come to this conclusion; everyone except FOX News.

Your so-called Intelligence Agencies, that look pretty stupid to me, are all part of the 'Deep State' out to destroy our great President.

And you're in a 'deep state' of denial if you believe that. Trump's own appointees verified that the Russians meddled in our election to help him win – including FBI Director, Christopher Wray, and former Director of National Intelligence, Dan Coats.

All part of the 'witch hunt.'

And I suppose you also believe that Clinton was running a child sex ring out of a pizza parlor.

That was all a joke. That's the trouble with you liberals. You take everything too seriously.

It was such a joke that someone showed up with an assault weapon to save the children—who were never there. These crazy conspiracy theories are fueled by people like Alex Jones--

Love him.

That's the problem. He spreads one bizarre made-up story after another, like the Newtown School massacre never happened. Do you really believe that all those dead children were just hoax actors?

Of course not. He went too far.

At last, something we agree on.

Chapter Seven:
FIRING BLANKS

But in his defense, Alex Jones was standing up for our gun rights. And there, he's right on target.

Okay, gun rights. Let me shoot my mouth off about that. We are the only country in the world - not in a war - that has this many gun fatalities. We average more than 35 to 40 thousand deaths a year – suicides, homicides, accidental deaths and mass shootings.

That's over a 100 people, on average, killed in this country every day.

It's unfortunate, but that's the price of freedom.

How about freedom from fear? When did it become normal for schools to hold active-shooter drills?

That's why we should arm teachers.

We shouldn't, and for a lot of reasons. For one, how would first-responders know the difference between the good guy and the bad guy. Second, there is no proof that arming teachers will stop shooters. Teachers are not trained to be policemen; they're trained to be educators. And I hope you're learning something!

Look, guns don't kill people. People kill people.

Bullets kill people, Uncle – especially when someone uses a weapon like the AR-15 designed for war, not self-defense. When assault weapons were banned from 1994 to 2004, high-fatality mass shootings dropped dramatically and then went way up when the ban expired.

Just admit it. Gun control is unconstitutional because you libs want to take our guns away. Justice Scalia said that.

Actually, Justice Scalia said you could keep a gun at home, but that the government could regulate firearms like military-style weapons. That would reduce the amount of gun violence. And if you need a license to drive a car, doesn't it make sense to have to be licensed to own a firearm? Countries, like Australia, that have healthy restrictions, have seen a dramatic drop in mass shootings, homicides and suicides.

The bottom line is that a good man with a gun can stop a bad man with a gun. That's why I have my gun rack over there and a pistol next to my bed, locked and loaded.

Just keep it locked until I go home, and don't use it when you're loaded. You are right that occasionally a citizen does stop a madman. But more often they could end up accidentally killing more people. Statistics show - more guns mean more violence.

It's not too many guns. It's too many crazy people.

Then why are you against background checks?

They won't work and we shouldn't penalize law-abiding citizens who want to purchase a gun for self-defense.

A short wait to legally buy a gun is not a burden to reduce the level of violence.

Violence? You're not looking at the real cause. It's those damn violent video games.

But that's nuts! There are crazy people and kids playing video games all over the world. The difference is they don't have access to guns the way Americans do. Game over.

You can shoot off your mouth all you want. But no matter what, the NRA says we need guns to keep the government from taking over and becoming a dictatorship.

The National Rifle Association has one purpose: to help gun manufacturers sell more guns, not represent gun owners. Remember, they're the ones who've been credibly accused of taking your dues and lining their own pockets, and do you think it is okay that the NRA took Russian rubles from Putin's lackey to help Trump get elected? And I'm surprised you're not upset about Maria Butina, the Russian spy who infiltrated the NRA.

We still need guns to prevent a tyrannical government. We are the well-armed militia that stands between freedom and slavery.

Look, Uncle, we still live in a democracy and we elect who runs the country. If we don't like them, we can vote them out and put someone else in charge. Our votes are the 'well-armed militia.' It's ballots...not bullets.

Chapter Eight

VOTER VICTIMS

Speaking of ballots, aren't you ashamed of all the voter fraud like the three million illegals that voted for Hillary?

Dios, mío, Uncle! If you believe that then you believe that Trump's inauguration was packed when photographs showed that he drew a much smaller crowd than Obama. There is absolutely no proof that voter fraud played any part in the election, unless you want to count the Russian interference. The only fraud is the ridiculous Voter

I.D. laws and the outrageously unfair gerrymandering used to suppress the minority vote. The truth be told, any voter fraud helped Trump and the Republicans, not Hillary.

Well, Trump got more votes.

He got more Electoral College votes, yes. But as I said earlier, almost 3 million more legitimate voters actually chose Hillary, which is why Trump makes up stories about voter fraud. He is embarrassed he got to be President even though he got fewer popular votes, which is why we should get rid of the Electoral College.

Are you kidding? We need the Electoral College so small states are treated fairly and not overlooked.

But they are being overlooked. The candidates ignore all but the so- called 11 'swing states' like Florida and Ohio. In the 2016 election, both candidates spent 2/3 of their time campaigning in those states. Also, would you like it if your vote was worth less because of where you live? Is that fair?

You're just a sore loser.

You bet I am, and I ain't the only one. This is the second time in 16 years where the Democrat got more popular votes and then the Republicans *stole the election. Remember Florida? Hanging chads? We got Bushwhacked. And now we have to put up with Trump and his crew who cheated as well.*

So what? We had to put up with Obama for eight years. A secret Muslim who wasn't even born here.

That nonsense again? Even Trump, the 'birther-in-chief', finally was forced to admit that Obama was born here. And he attended a Christian church in Chicago, not a mosque. So, what did you have to put up with? Obama saving the economy from the worst financial crisis since the Great Depression? Saving the auto industry? Giving you healthcare? Or cleaning up the environment? Or killing bin Laden?

What about all the corruption?

What corruption?

Benghazi! Fast and Furious! Just to name two.

The biggest non-scandal scandals to ever pollute our public discourse. Republicans held hearing after hearing, at our expense, and nothing ever came of it...because there was never anything there to begin with.

Obama and Clinton let innocent people die in Benghazi.

You really think they wanted them to die?

No, I didn't say that. But they should have had more security. And that's Clinton and Obama's fault. They ordered the security forces to stand down.

Where did you hear that?

Fox News.

Why am I not surprised? Guess what Uncle? The security forces got there as fast as they could. Even the Republican investigation confirms that. And did you know that House Republicans, who were in charge at the time, refused to fund hundreds of millions of dollars for diplomatic security before the attack? There's your scandal.

Chapter Nine

CORRUPTION ERUPTION

Well, at least we have a President now who is draining the swamp.

Yeah, the more he drains it, the more you can see the muck of corrupt Republicans at the bottom.

I'm sure you'll find some Democratic bottom-feeders down there as well. There's corruption on both sides.

It's not comparable. Republicans are way, way more corrupt than Democrats.

That's ridiculous. They're both equally corrupt.

Do the math. From 1961 to 2016, over 56 years. Democrats have held the Presidency for 28 and Republicans for 28. In that time, Democrats have had almost no scandals: 7 indicted, 3 convicted, one person went to prison. Now look at your Republicans: 126 indicted, 113 convicted, 39 sent to prison. Or put it this way, Republicans are 18 times more corrupt than Democrats; so, how can you say with a straight face that both sides are equally corrupt? Numbers don't lie.

You have your numbers, I have mine.

Like "alternative facts", you mean?

It's just a different perspective. You have your corruption, I have mine.

And Trump has his. Trump has several dozen ongoing investigations into his finances and for criminal behavior – on the federal and state level and in Congress.

Exactly. The Never-Trumpers want to discredit him and get him out of office. The 'Deep State' is out to get him.

What the hell is the 'Deep State?'

People in the government and military who are still bitter Hillary lost and will do anything to get rid of our great President and take control.

That's a shallow way of thinking. Do you really think a shadow government is out to get Trump?

You bet. They will do anything to get rid of him.

Who is 'they?' It's just an excuse to avoid facing the truth that Trump's National Security Advisor, Michael Flynn, pled guilty to lying to the FBI. Rick Gates, assistant campaign manager, also pled guilty to the same thing, and Paul Manafort, Trump's campaign manager, is in jail. Not to mention, Michael Cohen, Trump's lawyer in the Stormy Daniels cover up, who's also in the slammer – and campaign aide, George Papadopoulos, who also pled guilty for lying to the FBI, has already served his time. It goes on and on. It's like a bad reality show called "Prison Apprentice."

Chapter Ten:

PROS AT CONS

**You can make fun of "The Apprentice,"
but that show proved what a great
businessman and leader Trump is.**

*Then let's take a look at the 'real' reality.
Donald Trump is a failed tycoon who was*

continually bailed out by his rich old man. He's a guy who was born on third base and thinks he hit a triple.

But then he made his own fortune...on his own.

By going bankrupt six times? By stiffing one vendor after another? By hiring Polish workers to work on Trump Tower and then threatening to deport them when they wanted to get paid? That was reported in Time Magazine. I'm not making it up. How do you feel about that?

If they were illegal immigrants, they shouldn't have been working here in the first place.

And who do you think hired them?

Probably the construction foreman.

No, it was Trump himself. And many years later, he was forced to settle and pay the workers well over a million dollars.

Thank God he had the money. It's just doing business.

And how about Trump University, the scam school where he promised to teach poor suckers his secrets to success? He had to cough up 25 million bucks for that swindle.

They should have called the seminar, "The Art of Making the Steal."

That's not fair. He only settled because he didn't want anything interfering with his Presidency.

Sure, that's the reason. By the way, he's already been sued over a hundred times since he took office and let's not forget about the 3500 lawsuits he's been involved in before he was elected. And why won't he release his tax returns like he promised?

Because it's nobody's business.

It's everybody's business, actually.

Look, it will only show what a great businessman he is.

Yeah, a guy who lost over a billion dollars with his failed casinos and turned Atlantic City into a ghost town.

Even so, look at how he rebounded. He's a self-remade man and a role model for all ambitious Americans.

Are you sure of that? Maybe he doesn't want to show his taxes because he isn't nearly as rich as he claims or because his own lawyer has reported that he has committed tax fraud by inflating and deflating his assets when it helps him.

Well, you can't make an omelet without breaking some eggs. And that's why we need him in the White House. He's bringing business back to America.

And he's bringing diplomats to his DC hotel - and profiting off his own foreign holdings at the same time by 'encouraging' the Air Force to stay at his Scottish Golf Resort. This is not to mention the Saudis who partied at the same place with their 100 pieces of luggage. And his eldest kids are following in his footsteps and enriching themselves through dubious business arrangements.

Liberals are just jealous. Donald Trump knows business because he comes from a long line of successful businessmen. It's in his genes.

Can't argue with that. His grandfather, Frederick Drumpf, was a pimp, tax evader and draft dodger. Sound familiar? And his father was a racist and a member of the Ku Klux Klan - who was sued by the U.S. government, along with Donald, for refusing to rent to African-Americans.

Chapter Eleven:

THE FOUNDING FOOLERS

Look nobody's perfect. We all have skeletons in our closet. But Trump is an instrument of God, putting good Christian

conservatives on the court and in the government.

Are you saying that Trump is a good Christian in spite of his womanizing and purported sexual assaults?

I read my Bible! Trump is like King Cyrus of Persia who helped the Jews even though he wasn't Jewish himself.

That's because he liked Gefilte Fish.

You can make fun if you want, but Trump was divinely chosen to restore the Christian Dominion in America.

What are you talking about? America was never meant to be a Christian nation. It's in the constitution. "Congress shall make no law respecting the establishment of religion." Not once is God mentioned in our founding document. Not once!

Yes, but our founders were all Christian.

Oh, my God! You have to be kidding. Many of the founding fathers were Deists who did not believe in the supernatural aspects of Christian teachings but more in the realities of nature and the universe. John Adams, our second President, said, "The government of the United States is not, in any sense, founded on the Christian religion."

Nonsense. The majority of this country has always been God-fearing Christians and always will be. But if it were up to you, there would be no Christ in Christmas!

You mean the phony 'War on Christmas?'

You bet! Nobody says 'Merry Christmas' anymore. They have to say 'Happy Holidays', like Obama.

Obama said "Merry Christmas" many times. Just go on YouTube. And in fact, the only time that Christmas was actually banned in America was by the Puritans in 1659 because they considered it a sinful and superstitious celebration. That was the real war on Christmas!

Chapter Twelve:

SIDING WITH THE WRONG SIDE

I'll tell you what the real war is. It's murderous Muslims and their Sharia law aimed at destroying the Christians…and the Jews!

You're right, Uncle. There is a problem with 'fundamentalist Muslims' who want to create a Caliphate and convert everyone to Islam. And there are fanatical Jihadists who will blow themselves up so they can get their 72 virgins.

I'm glad you see the problem.

I do. But I don't agree with the solution. By invading Iraq, we created ISIS. We are buddy buddy with Saudi Arabia even though most of the 9/11 hijackers came from there - and Osama Bin Laden was also a Saudi. Both George W. Bush and Donald J. Trump have given them a pass on everything. And Trump has been kissing up to Prince Mohammed bin Salman who had journalist Jamal Khashoggi, an American resident, murdered and dismembered. Could it be because the Saudis are heavily invested in Trump's properties?

Sometimes you have to work with people who are less than perfect to stop another terrorist attack on our soil.

Soil that is soaked in the blood of numberless innocents murdered by home-grown terrorists, not Muslims. Right-wing extremists, nationalists, Neo-Nazis and white supremacists have been responsible for more mass murders in the last year since Timothy McVeigh blew up the Federal Building in Oklahoma.

Okay, but remember, evil is everywhere and you got to be on your guard.

That's true, but you can't be in denial of what is going on, like our President, who says that in Charlottesville, "There were good people on both sides." Good people, like the white supremacist who ran over that poor young lady at the protests?

That was just terrible, but that wasn't Trump's fault. He didn't advocate violence. He was just defending people who want to preserve our American heritage.

You mean the Confederate flag and statues that glorify racism and slavery?

It's a noble heritage, with heroes who fought on both sides.

Only if you consider traitors "heroes". Did you know that the creator of the Confederate flag, William T. Thompson, back in 1863, said: "As a people we are fighting to maintain the heaven-ordained supremacy of the white man over the inferior or colored race."

There is nothing noble about glorifying racism, which your 'fearful leader' does on a daily basis.

Donald Trump is not a racist. You just can't accept that he's not politically correct.

You're right. He's not politically correct. He's politically corrupt. He relies on racism to scare and divide the country. He advertised in the New York Times for the Central Park Five to be executed, and then wouldn't admit he was wrong even after they were exonerated. He trashes places like Puerto Rico, Haiti and African nations as "shithole countries" and wishes we had more immigrants from Norway!

It is as clear as black and white.

May I remind you that Lincoln was a Republican and it was the Southern Democrats who opposed civil rights!

And that is the Democrats' shame, but then they became the party of Civil Rights, while the Republicans' Southern Strategy helped them win by appealing to bigotry in 1968. Strom Thurmond? Spiro Agnew? Remember them? Lincoln would be turning over in his grave.

Chapter Thirteen

MONKEY BUSINESS

TRICKLE DOWN IS MONKEY BUSINESS!

No, Lincoln would be proud of Republicans today. Trump has created more jobs for blacks than any other President.

No, he hasn't. Obama created well over a million more jobs than Trump.

Well, you can't deny that the economy is booming.

Most of that has to do with policies of the Obama Administration, which dug us out of the worst financial nightmare since the Great Depression.

You just don't want to give Trump credit.

If you want to talk about credit, think of the millions of hard-working Americans whose credit cards are maxed out – trying to survive week to week. Over 50% of working adults can't afford to miss one paycheck and 40% of Americans would be devastated by even a $400 emergency.

But look at the stock market.

Fine. Let's look at it. Most Americans don't own stock and 84% of stocks are owned by the wealthiest 10%.

Oh, that's rich.

Like you, Uncle.

I wish!

Look, the rich are getting richer, and everyone else is trying to stay above water. The top 1% of the super-rich own 40% of the country's wealth - more than the bottom 90% combined. If we could make things a little fairer, everybody would be better off.

Not the rich.

Oh, they'll get by.

What screws up the economy is all the wasteful spending and huge deficits run up by the Democrats!

Huge deficits by the Dems?! Now you've opened up a barrelful of monkeys. If Trump keeps on going at this rate, his budgets would increase the debt to 29 Trillion Dollars. That's a lot of cheeseburgers.

He's just trying to juice the economy.

By putting the squeeze on guys like you! He cut taxes for his rich buddies and promised us it wouldn't increase the deficit!

You don't get it, do you? Those tax cuts will trickle down to everyone else.

Like a golden shower from a Russian whore?

Hey! Show some respect! That's our President you're talking about.

Seriously, Uncle, ever since Reagan, the GOP has enacted 'Trickle Down Economics' - which the first President Bush called 'Voodoo Economics' by the way. In the Reagan, Bush I, Bush II and Trump's administrations the deficits went through the roof.

Face it - the only time Republicans care about the deficit is when there is a Democrat in the White House.

You're forgetting that by removing all the unnecessary and crazy regulations, businesses will boom and we'll blow away the deficit.

Good idea. Let's start burning more coal, fracking wherever we can, and drilling in our beautiful national parks. That will "Make America Great Again."

You can be as sarcastic as you want, but that'll make us energy independent and put a lot of fine people to work.

Despite right-wing distortions, the 'Green New Deal' could put even more people to work and create a world with much less pollution. They estimate 24 million new jobs worldwide with a good percentage of those right at home in the U.S.A.! In fact, the green economy is creating 1.3 trillion dollars in yearly sales and 9.5 million jobs here already. That's good business and we'd be saving our country and the planet at the same time.

Okay, here we go. That climate change, global warming hoax. You lefties just want to control everything we do, including what kind of straws we suck on.

I tell you what sucks. The Trump administration is hiding the fact that 97% of scientists agree that we are in serious jeopardy and unless we do something dramatic, we may already be too late. We've just had the hottest five years in recorded history. Hurricanes, tornadoes, blizzards and floods are getting stronger and more frequent. Forest fires are raging all over the planet. I know you care about your grandkids, right? You can't deny it anymore.

It's a natural cycle.

It's not natural for glaciers to be melting at such an alarming rate. This is not a liberal or conservative issue. It is a human issue.

There is no plan B if our planet becomes uninhabitable. I think we all agree that clean air, clean water, and clean food is something we all want.

Chapter Fourteen:
CONCEPTION DECEPTION

OH, BABY!

I'll tell you what's going to do us in before that. The Muslims are making all the babies now, while we're killing babies with abortions.

First of all, I'm not sure about your facts regarding Muslims. And for your information, there are fewer abortions now in the U.S.A. than any time since Roe vs. Wade.

One is too many because you're murdering an innocent child.

You're missing the point. This is an issue about tissue. Can a cluster of cells in a woman's body really be considered a fully formed human being? There's no heart, no lungs, no brain. It's a no-brainer.

That's not funny. It has the potential to be a human being and deserves the chance to develop.

Even if the pregnancy is the result of rape or incest?

God works in mysterious ways.

Maybe. But God is not the one who has to carry the child to term and then raise it.

And that's why God made women.

So, you're saying that women are responsible no matter what?

No, it takes a man to impregnate a woman. Both of them should be more careful.

Then why are you so against Planned Parenthood?

Because they kill babies and sell the body parts. It's an abortion factory.

More fake news, Uncle. Abortions only make up 3% of the services and late-term abortions are only used to save the life of the mother or because the fetus would not survive. Most of Planned Parenthood's work is women's healthcare, cancer screenings and contraception.

A lot of that contraception stuff may as well be abortion. Justice Clarence Thomas said that.

But Uncle, that's just not true. If your goal is to stop unwanted pregnancies, which we both want, then you should be supporting Planned Parenthood, not condemning it.

Chapter Fifteen:
ABSTINENCE MAKES THE
HARD GROW LONGER

The problem is that they're teaching kids about sex, and they're watching the porn on the Internet.

I agree, Uncle, that kids shouldn't be learning about sex from watching porn. That's very unhealthy. That's why giving youngsters proper information about sex and love and contraception and abstinence is good for them.

I'll go with that abstinence thing.

Oh, really? That's not what Aunt Lydia said.

Very funny. Let me tell you something, kid. What happens in the bedroom, stays in the bedroom. The real problem is that you liberals are treating adults like children and children like adults.

FYI, statistics show that conservative schools that emphasize abstinence-only education have a higher rate of teen pregnancies. Look, people are warned never to drink and drive - but we don't tell them not to drive. Giving teenagers information about sex is not telling them to have sex, but it helps prevent disease and unwanted pregnancies.

But they're also teaching them that it's okay to have homosexual relations. That's an abomination and a sin. It's in the Bible.

The Bible says lots of stuff, but don't you agree that Jesus taught us two main things...to love God, and to love others as you would love yourself?

I agree with everything Jesus said, but in Leviticus it says, "If a man lies with another man as if with a woman, he shall be put to death."

But it doesn't say anything about a woman lying with another woman.

Because that's hot.

And sexist, too, Uncle.

Ahh, I'm just joking. That's immoral, too.

You have to admit times have changed.

For the worst. This Gay Marriage thing is being jammed down our throats.

Why do you say that? If two men or two women get married, it doesn't affect you in the least.

Oh, no? The next thing will be people marrying their pets.

Like Fido? Who cuddles up with you and Aunt Lydia every night?

That's just a ménagerie à trois. Listen, God made Adam and Eve, not Adam and Steve.

But we're all equal in the eyes of God, right? If God didn't love LGBTQ people, and didn't want them to find love, too - he wouldn't have created them.

Chapter Sixteen:
SUPREMELY SUBJECTIVE

But it's out of control! Gay Marriage, Roe versus Wade, – that's why we need strict constructionists on the Supreme Court who will honor the constitution.

Let me ask you a question. What does strict constructionism mean?

Well, it means doing what the constitution says, like what Justice Scalia wanted.

Okay. But if the constitution is always correct, why would you need a Supreme Court to begin with?

Well, to figure out what it means.

Exactly. That's the whole point. That's why there is no such thing as a strict constructionist. It's just a term conservatives use to justify whatever ruling they make. It's sort of like when someone quotes the Bible. People interpret the Bible differently and the same thing is true of the Constitution.

You just don't like that the conservative justices don't make up laws like you liberals do.

Well, let's see who makes up laws. How about Bush v. Gore where they stopped the recount. Do you think the conservative justices would have stopped the counting of votes if Gore had been ahead?

That again? Hanging chads. What nonsense.

But Uncle, wouldn't you have been enraged if they had done that to Bush?

The Supreme Court is protecting the rights of the people.

Like with Citizen's United, which argues that corporations are people too – and allows corporations to spend unlimited amounts on political campaigns? Yet, isn't it funny they won't hold corporate leaders responsible for lying - like the tobacco companies? Statistics show that most of the decisions the Supreme Court makes favor big business over people. Can you tell me what part of the constitution that's from?

They're just trying to keep us from becoming a socialist nanny-state. Look at Bernie Sanders. He wants to give everyone free college tuition and forgive student debts.

There are over two dozen countries all over the world that offer free college education - from Finland to Uruguay; and we have free education through high school. You went to public schools. Don't you think that's good?

Of course. I learned how to make lamps in wood shop, and you're sitting under one.

Well, there you go. That's Democratic Socialism. And don't you agree that society is better off when people are educated?

Yes, but I don't want to pay for it.

You're paying for it anyway, Uncle. Do you really want to keep on supporting people who are unskilled and unemployable and end up on welfare? And what about the G.I. Bill that got Grandpa his degree? An educated society pays for itself in the long run.

You just want to fill young people's heads with liberal hogwash.

They call it 'liberal arts'. It has nothing to do with politics.

Oh, really? Then why are all these Conservatives being banned from speaking

on campuses? Everyone should be allowed to speak.

I agree. Sometimes, political correctness goes too far.

Wow! I can't believe you agree with me again.

That's why all this tribal stuff is unhealthy, Uncle. We're not just liberals or conservatives. We're all Americans and we're all in this together, aren't we?

I suppose. But some of us are more American than others.

How do you know who is more American?

Well, people who have been here the longest and remember how good things used to be.

So would you say that Native Americans are the most American then? They've been here the longest, before immigrants put them on reservations.

That was justified. They were savages.

They were victims. How would you like your land taken from you?

It wouldn't have happened if they were good Christians to begin with.

You want to put me on a reservation? I'm not a Christian.

What are you talking about?

I don't practice any religion, but I believe in God, just like you.

It's that attitude that allows the persecution of us Christians.

If Christians are being persecuted, then why are churches tax-exempt, why are right-wing evangelical preachers allowed to preach politics?

Because of the First Amendment and because our country has lost its morality.

You don't have to be religious to be moral. Some of the most outspoken religious leaders are the biggest hypocrites, like Jim Bakker and Judge Roy Moore. They think that just because they pray, they can prey on other people.

Chapter Eighteen:

REGULATING REGULATORS

There are rotten apples in every barrel.

Yeah, the bottom of the barrel. Just look at the people who make up Trump's base: they're all Red, White and Blue.

Damn right!

WHITE-skinned RED-necks suffering from a bad case of BLUE-balls.

Now, wait a minute. That's deplorable.

Damn right!

And I suppose your pot-smoking Hollywood loudmouth liberals are not deplorable?

What's really deplorable are all the crooks and criminals that Trump has surrounded himself with from the campaign to now.

Like who?

I already mentioned some of the people who were indicted - or went to jail. Did I mention felon Roger Stone who conspired with WikiLeaks? Uncle, don't you think there's something wrong with a guy who gets a giant tattoo of Richard Nixon on his back?

Well, it's not something I would do, but just look at all the great people Trump put in his cabinet.

And I wish they'd stay in there. Do you remember Tom Price, his first Secretary of Human Resources, who had to resign because of illegal stock trades?

That's just one example...

Of many. Shall I go on? Ryan Zinke, the former Secretary of the Interior who had to resign for ethics issues. And do you think it was acceptable for Scott Pruitt, the head of the Environmental Protection Agency, to fly all over the country in private jets at our expense, request a bulletproof SUV, and install a $43,000 soundproof phone booth in his office? Why didn't he just use the 'cone of silence' like Agent 86, Maxwell Smart?

Scott Pruitt at least got rid of a lot of job-killing EPA regulations.

The truth is that there is no evidence that these regulations cost jobs. They do cost businesses some money, like the oil companies, but they can afford it. And we already agreed we all want to drink clean water, and breathe clear air.

And I suppose you're against clean coal and putting the coal miners back to work.

There is no such thing as clean coal, which spews huge amounts of toxic cyanide gas in the air. And because of natural gas and renewable energy, coal is becoming obsolete, anyway. We need to retrain miners for the modern energy sources like solar and wind.

What happens if the wind stops blowing or the sun stops shining right in the middle of the World Series? The TV is gonna go black in the last of the ninth inning. How about that?

Well, that's just silly. I'd say put it where the sun don't shine.

Oh, yeah! Eat my shorts.

Only if they're biodegradable. Look, we're talking about the 'Green Economy' here, and just like grass, it's going to keep growing. Scientists are working on battery technology so that more energy can be stored more easily. Once it's fully developed, we will never run out and it will be incredibly cheap and won't pollute the air.

Chapter Nineteen:

GOING TO POT

I'll tell you what's polluting the air. All that legal pot you and your hippie friends are smoking. And it's polluting your minds, too.

Sure, some people use cannabis to relax or get high. But a lot of people, like Aunt Eunice, needed it when she was doing chemotherapy. You approved of that, didn't you?

Sure. She was sick and it was part of her treatment.

And you wouldn't want her arrested for doing that, would you?

Don't be ridiculous.

And you have to admit, marijuana is no worse than alcohol and tobacco. And you could argue it's actually healthier than both of those. Look at all the problems we have now with teenagers who are vaping.

Pot is a gateway to harder drugs.

Most people who use pot do not go on to harder drugs. When you were smoking a pack a day, did you go out and buy a box of cigars?

I hate the smell of cigars.

There you go. Putting people in jail for smoking pot, most of whom are nonviolent, is just wrong – and costing taxpayers, like you and me, a bundle.

It's still a federal crime. They're breaking the law.

This whole war on drugs thing is just a smokescreen to justify the imprisonment of minorities. Look at the sentences blacks get for smoking crack cocaine compared to privileged whites who just put the powder up their nose. It's unfair and absurd.

There you go, playing the race card again.

Yeah, the human race. Don't you agree that putting people in jail for having addictions is unjust? We should be trying to treat them, not punish them.

If you do the crime, you should do the time.

Except too often the rich and well connected get away with murder, sometimes literally, while the poor and poorly represented are sent to the slammer.

If you ask me, there should be more in prison, like those football players who won't stand for the national anthem.

You really think Colin Kaepernick should be in jail?

Maybe not. But anybody that unpatriotic shouldn't be allowed to play.

Not for the Patriots, maybe. He wasn't disrespecting the flag, but just drawing attention to police brutality against blacks.

The NFL is a private business. They can do what they want.

That's true. But they sure seem to be okay with allowing wife-beaters and drug users on the field. They came down on Kaepernick because they were intimidated by Trump.

Thank God we have a President who stands up for the flag.

And takes a knee to Putin and the Saudis.

The Saudis have been our allies for years. And they sure don't need a handout from Uncle Sam - while everyone else has their hands out.

Like Jared Kushner? And President Trump? The Saudis have been oiling their palms for years!

What's the problem? They're businessmen looking for investors.

The problem is that Trump wants to make deals with the biggest thugs on the planet like Putin, North Korea's Kim Jong Un, and that murderous nutcase in the Philippines, Rodrigo Duterte. Meanwhile, he is alienating all our real allies like Germany, France and Great Britain.

He does that because those countries are not paying their fair share.

Even if that is occasionally true, we shouldn't be dumping on our friends who are democracies like we are. We give foreign aid to make America safer. The money we spend, like for NATO, is much cheaper in the long run than paying for more wars.

They should pay for their own wars. They've been relying on us for far too long. Like the Ukraine. Hell, we just gave them 400 million dollars.

Yeah, with a few strings attached, which makes their President Zelensky look like a puppet.

You going to bring up that hoax, or as I like to say, 'witch hunt' number two.

And number three, and number four and number five. Which hunt are we talking about?

Any one of them. They're all designed to discredit and disrespect our President, and negate the votes of millions of Americans who put him in office.

Come on, Uncle. You do know that it is illegal to get a foreign country's help in an election, and that's just what Trump was trying to do. He wouldn't release the money Congress appropriated for Ukraine's defense unless they made up lies about Joe Biden and his son. And then Trump, Pence, Barr, and Giuliani tried to cover it up.

What's really being covered up is Biden's bad boy, Hunter, who made 50 grand a month for doing nothing.

You know, Biden's son admits that taking that gig was unwise, even though it has been established there was nothing criminal about it. But it was no more shady than Ivanka's trademark deals with the Chinese, and Don Jr. and Eric Trump's business deals all over the world.

Except that Joe Biden got the prosecutor fired who was out to expose Hunter's corruption.

In fact, the opposite is true. The prosecutor in question was corrupt himself and was being paid off NOT TO PROSECUTE corruption. Vice President Biden, The World Bank, and the rest of the European Union – not to mention some of your favorite Republican Senators like Ron Johnson and Rob Porter - demanded that prosecutor be fired.

Chapter Twenty-One:

HYPOCRITICAL HYPOCRITES

The bottom line is that you just don't want to accept that **Donald Trump is a great leader and is pursuing the truth,** which you can't take.

What I can't take is that Donald Trump believes that the Constitution grants him the powers of a king. And that's the truth you can't take. Doesn't that bother you?

What bothers me is that you won't give him any credit for anything, like our great economy. Look at the unemployment rate!

I'll agree that the unemployment rate has gone down. That's good. But a lot of those folks are working part-time or need more than one job to survive. And remember, the people who have stopped looking are not included in these statistics.

As I said, you won't give him credit for anything.

Like Trump won't give Obama credit for leaving him such a robust economy when he took office.

Oh, your great saint, Barack Hussein Obama. The man who could do no wrong.

He did plenty of things wrong. But I suppose what bothers me the most, is the double standards.

That's doubletalk. What do you mean?

Let's try a thought experiment, Uncle. How would you feel if Barack Obama had done or said the following?

Tried to get other countries to make up lies about Mitt Romney, his opponent in the 2012 election, or asked Russia to hack into his emails like Trump requested when he said, "Russia, if you're listening..."

Paid off a porn star and a playmate to keep his affairs secret.

Had his aides meet secretly with Russian agents.

Declared himself chosen by God.

Spent one-third of his time in office at one his hotels or golf courses.

Said it's okay to "grab women by the pussy."

Been accused of assaulting more than 20 women.

Encourages people to ignore subpoenas and labels those who defy him as "traitors and spies".

Wanted to invite the Taliban to Camp David.

Labeled the loyal opposition as hate-driven liars.

Called for the exposure of a whistleblower.

Held secret meetings with foreign leaders.

Ran a shadow foreign policy through his personal lawyer, Rudy Giuliani.

Stated that John McCain, who spent years being tortured in a Hanoi prison, wasn't a war hero because he was captured.

Publicly ridiculed the parents of another war hero (the Khans).

Avoided service in Vietnam by claiming he had bone spurs, but couldn't remember in what foot.

Asserted that avoiding STDs was his Vietnam.

Dictated his own doctor's letter to say he is, "the healthiest individual ever elected to the presidency."

Bragged to the Boy Scouts that as a young man he went to a hot New York party on a yacht.

Proclaimed he believes Vladimir Putin over his own intelligence agencies.

Asserted that Saudi Arabian Crown Prince Mohammed bin Salman had nothing to do with the murder of journalist Jamal Khashoggi when it is obvious that he ordered him to be hacked to death.

Refused to release his tax returns after promising numerous times he would.

Insisted that Hurricane Dorian was going to hit Alabama and used a Sharpie to edit the path of the storm - even after he was corrected by the National Weather Service.

Claimed the noise from wind turbines causes cancer.

Said he wanted to ban electricity efficient light bulbs because they make him look orange.

Said about Megyn Kelly that there was "blood coming out of her wherever."

Claimed that he donated one million dollars to veterans until it was revealed he hadn't.

Had his charitable foundation fined two million dollars for fraud.

Tried and then failed to get the next G-7 to take place at his own hotel so he could make a profit.

Continually makes up derogatory names like an eight-year-old bully for his opponents: like

"Sleepy Joe" and "Crooked Hillary" and "Shifty Schiff."

Physically mocked a disabled reporter at a rally.

Uses obscenities on public media.

Bans reporters from his press conferences.

Calls the news media "the enemy of the people."

Withdrew our troops from the Middle East without consulting his generals while betraying our allies the Kurds who helped us fight ISIS.

Pardoned war criminals.

Declared a national emergency to build a border wall.

Diverted vital funds from federal programs and the military to build that wall.

Reportedly considered adding a moat on the border filled with alligators and snakes.

Called himself a "stable genius."

Started a ridiculous trade war with China that is bankrupting farmers and other businesses.

Took actions to undermine our commitment to NATO.

Wrote love letters to Kim Jong Un, the dictator of North Korea - and kisses the ass of every sociopathic strongman he meets.

Enough already. You made your point. You're in your world...and I'm in mine.

I'm afraid that's true. But you know what Uncle? I still love you.

And in spite of the fact that you're so wrong, I love you, too.

Well, after dishing all this dirt, I hope you and I have at least found a little common ground. It would be really nice if we could find a way to talk like this more often. After all, we are family.

I agree, and I'm thirsty. You want a beer?

Sure. But, uh, what should we talk about?

Sports - of course!

BIBLIOGRAPHY

Foreword

https://www.smh.com.au/politics/federal/cancer-eating-the-heart-of-australian-democracy-20180826-p4zzum.html

Chapter 1 – Liar in Chief

ABA - https://www.americanbar.org/news/abanews/aba-news-archives/2019/03/mueller-concludes-investigation/

Wikipedia - Veracity of Statements by Donald Trump

https://en.wikipedia.org/wiki/Veracity_of_statements_by_Donald_T rump

Chicago Tribune - April 4, 2019

https://www.chicagotribune.com/nation-world/ct-trump-russia-mueller-report-mainstream-media-20190419-story.html

Chapter 2 – Kids in Cages

Ana Campoy, Quartz - March 14, 2018

https://qz.com/1227461/trumps-immigration-claims-debunked-texas-data-show-us-born-americans-commit-more-rape-and-murder/

David Bier, Cato Institute - July 3, 2019

https://www.cato.org/blog/77-drug-traffickers-are-us-citizens-not-illegal-immigrants

Michelle Ye Hee Lee, Washington Post - July 8, 2015

https://www.washingtonpost.com/news/fact-checker/wp/2015/07/08/donald-trumps-false-comments-connecting-mexican-immigrants-and-crime/?noredirect=on

PBS - February 8, 2019

https://www.pbs.org/newshour/politics/ap-fact-check-trump-plays-on-immigration-myths

Julia Preston, NY Times – September 21, 2016

https://www.nytimes.com/2016/09/22/us/immigrants-arent-taking-americans-jobs-new-study-finds.html

Various Sources for ADL.org

https://www.adl.org/resources/fact-sheets/myths-and-facts-about-immigrants-and-immigration-en-espanol

Rick Jervis, USA Today – June 20, 2018

https://www.usatoday.com/story/news/nation/2018/06/20/family-separation-us-border-trump-immigrant-children/712687002/

Chapter 3 – White on White

Kimberly Amadeo, The Balance – August 27, 2019

https://www.thebalance.com/welfare-programs-definition-and-list-3305759

Michael Harriot, The Root – June 22, 2018

https://www.theroot.com/the-oppression-of-white-america-1827018691

Chapter 4 – The Commies are Coming

ObamaCareFacts.coming ObamaCare Opinions, Op-ed, and Other Articles - March 30, 2015, Last Updated - March 28, 2016 https://obamacarefacts.com/2015/03/30/why-obamacare-is-not-socialism/

Niran S. Al-Agba, MD, KevinMD – May 9, 2019

https://www.kevinmd.com/blog/2019/05/medicare-for-all-doesnt-look-like-single-payer-in-the-rest-of-the-world.html

Arthur Delaney and Alissa Scheller, HuffPost – February 28, 2015

https://www.huffpost.com/entry/food-stamp-demographics_n_6771938

Author Unknown – Medicare for All, DSA

https://medicareforall.dsausa.org/organizing-guide/socialism-and-medicare-for-all

Jake Johnson, Common Dreams – June 6, 2019

https://www.commondreams.org/news/2019/06/14/eye-popping-analysis-shows-top-1-gained-21-trillion-wealth-1989-while-bottom-half?utm_campaign=shareaholic&utm_medium=referral&utm_source=email_this

Chapter 5 – Collusion Confusion

Zack Beauchamp, Vox – April 18, 2019

https://www.vox.com/2019/4/18/18484965/mueller-report-trump-no-collusion

ABA- March 2019

https://www.americanbar.org/news/abanews/aba-news-archives/2019/03/mueller-concludes-investigation/

Julian Shen-Berro – HuffPost – July 24, 2019

https://www.huffpost.com/entry/mueller-testimony-exoneration_n_5d38621be4b0419fd33617c3

Chapter 6 – Which Witch is Which

Snopes – July 20, 2017

https://www.snopes.com/fact-check/hillary-bill-clinton-russia-sanctions-speech/

Tucker Higgins, CNBC – September 15, 2018

https://www.cnbc.com/2018/09/14/alex-jones-5-most-disturbing-ridiculous-conspiracy-theories.html

RevealNews in collaboration with Rolling Stone and Type Investigations - Nov. 18, 2017.

https://www.revealnews.org/episodes/pizzagate-a-slice-of-fake-news-rebroadcast/

Abigail Abrams, Time - April 18, 2019

https://time.com/5565991/russia-influence-2016-election/

Chapter 7 – Firing Blanks

Michael Shammas, HuffPost – October 13, 2017

https://www.huffpost.com/entry/its-time-to-retire-the-guns-dont-kill-people-people_b_59e0f6d4e4b09e31db975887

Jay Michaelson, Daily Beast – August 13, 2019

https://www.thedailybeast.com/even-supreme-court-justice-antonin-scalia-would-allow-todays-gun--proposals-after-el-paso-and-dayton

Christopher Ingraham, Washington Post - July 27, 2018

https://www.washingtonpost.com/business/2018/07/27/actually-guns-do-kill-people-according-new-study/

Alex Yablon, The Trace - August 16, 2019

https://www.thetrace.org/2019/08/what-the-data-says-asssault-weapons-bans/

David Welna, NPR – April 8, 2013

https://www.npr.org/sections/itsallpolitics/2013/04/08/176350364/fears-of-government-tyranny-push-some-to-reject-gun-control

Anonymous, Amnesty.org

https://www.amnesty.org/en/what-we-do/arms-control/gun-violence/

Anonymous, Giffords Law Center

https://lawcenter.giffords.org/gun-laws/policy-areas/background-checks/universal-background-checks/

Meghan Keneally, ABC News, October 29, 2018

https://abcnews.go.com/US/breaking-nra-backed-theory-good-guy-gun-stops/story?id=53360480

Katie Beck, BBC News, Sydney – October 4, 2017

https://www.bbc.com/news/world-australia-35048251

Nick Evershed, The Guardian – March 19, 2019

https://www.theguardian.com/news/datablog/2019/mar/20/strict-firearm-laws-reduce-gun-deaths-heres-the-evidence

https://www.omicsonline.org/open-access/guns-and-games-the-relationship-between-violent-video-games-andgun-crimes-in-america-2151-6200-1000207.php?aid=77854

Carla K. Johnson, AP News - August 5, 2019

https://www.apnews.com/b8ce29d88543479bbd4894f5a39cc686

Alex Yablon, Vice - July 2, 2017

https://www.vice.com/en_us/article/evd4we/the-good-guy-with-a-gun-theory-debunked

Mike Colagrossi, Big Think – August 17, 2019

https://bigthink.com/politics-current-affairs/gun-violence-mental-illness?rebelltitem=3#rebelltitem3

Chapter 8 – Voter Victims

Andrew Prokop, Vox - December 19, 2016

https://www.vox.com/policy-and-politics/2016/11/7/12315574/electoral-college-explained-presidential-elections-2016

Reed E. Hunt, Salon – February 4, 2019

https://www.salon.com/2019/02/04/who-gets-hurt-worst-by-the-electoral-college-its-not-democrats-its-democracy/

ProCon.org – September 1, 2019

https://www.procon.org/headline.php?headlineID=005330

Angie Drobnic Holan, Politifact - August 26, 2010

https://www.politifact.com/truth-o-meter/article/2010/aug/26/why-do-so-many-people-think-obama-muslim/

Loren Collins, Bullspotting

http://www.bullspotting.com/articles/the-secret-origins-of-birtherism/

Yoni Appelbaum, The Atlantic - March 2019

https://www.theatlantic.com/magazine/archive/2019/03/impeachm
ent-trump/580468/

Joel Mathis, The Week - August 22, 2019

https://theweek.com/articles/860447/astounding-unrelenting-
foolishness-president-trump

Chapter 9 - Corruption Eruption

Jen Psaki, CNN - October 3, 2017

https://www.cnn.com/2017/10/03/opinions/trump-swamp-monster-
opinion-psaki/index.html

Emma Roller, Splinter News – June 15, 2018

https://splinternews.com/a-list-of-all-the-insanely-corrupt-shit-
scott-pruitt-ha-1826864212

David Leonhardt and Ian Prasad Philbrick, New York Times-
October 18, 2018

https://www.nytimes.com/2018/10/28/opinion/trump-
administration-corruption-conflicts.html

Joan Walsh Twitter, The Nation – August 28, 2019

https://www.thenation.com/article/donald-trump-corruption-william-
barr-g-7-doral/

Chapter 10 - Pros At Cons

Russ Buettner and Susanne Craig, NY Times, May 5, 2019

https://www.nytimes.com/interactive/2019/05/07/us/politics/donald
-trump-taxes.html

Tim King, American Herald Tribune – December 11, 2015

https://ahtribune.com/us/2016-election/242-trump-grandfather-pimp-father-kkk.html?fbclid=IwAR0tyLjn-k6PYNZzhygHykqGfIDgxJCpo6uZBIX2tXVJ-C1KUHoldu-J7Zg

Massimo Calabresi, Time - August 25, 2016

https://time.com/4465744/donald-trump-undocumented-workers/

https://time.com/4343030/donald-trump-failures/

Chapter 11- The Founding Foolers

Tara Isabella Burton, Vox - March 5, 2018

https://www.vox.com/identities/2018/3/5/16796892/trump-cyrus-christian-right-bible-cbn-evangelical-propaganda

Jessie Blaeser, The Tylt – November 2018

https://thetylt.com/culture/christmas-war

Jeff Schweitzer, HuffPost - April 28, 2015

https://m.huffpost.com/us/entry/us_6761840?guccounter=1

Russell Shorto, New York Times – February 11, 2010

https://www.nytimes.com/2010/02/14/magazine/14texbooks-t.html

Chapter 12 - Siding With the Wrong Side

Jack Shafer, Politico Magazine – July 15, 2019
https://www.politico.com/magazine/story/2019/07/15/donald-trump-is-who-we-thought-he-was-227358

R. Muse, Politicus USA – July 3, 2015

https://www.politicususa.com/2015/07/03/confederate-flag-designer-symbol-white-supremacy-southern-heritage.html

Vera Bergengruen and W.J. Hennigan, Time - August 8, 2019

https://time.com/5647304/white-nationalist-terrorism-united-states/

https://en.wikipedia.org/wiki/Timothy_McVeigh

Chapter 13 - Monkey Business

Linda Qiu, New York Times – August 14, 2018

https://www.nytimes.com/2018/08/14/us/politics/fact-check-trump-jobs-black-americans.html

Jonathan Chait, New York Magazine – August 20, 2019

http://nymag.com/intelligencer/2019/08/gop-suspects-economic-sabotage-because-they-did-it-to-obama.html

The Times Editorial Board, The Times – August 23, 2019

https://www.latimes.com/opinion/story/2019-08-22/trump-deficit-democratic-candidates

Christopher Ingraham, Washington Post – December 6, 2017

https://www.washingtonpost.com/news/wonk/wp/2017/12/06/the-richest-1-percent-now-owns-more-of-the-countrys-wealth-than-at-any-time-in-the-past-50-years/

Pippa Stevens, CNBC – October 16, 2019

https://www.cnbc.com/2019/10/16/us-green-economy-generates-1point3-trillion-and-employs-millions-new-study-finds.html?__source=facebook%7Cmain

Mark Schmitt, Vox - April 20, 2018

https://www.vox.com/polyarchy/2018/4/20/17262944/democrats-fiscal-responsibility-budget-deficits

Nick Hanauer, The American Prospect – June 26, 2018

https://prospect.org/article/want-expand-economy-tax-rich

Manny Otiko, Medium - September 24, 2018

https://medium.com/datadriveninvestor/trickle-down-economics-doesnt-work-so-why-do-republicans-keep-trying-it-3987459108b5

UN.org -April 3, 2019

https://www.un.org/sustainabledevelopment/blog/2019/04/green-economy-could-create-24-million-new-jobs/

Jonathan Hahn, Sierra Club - November 26, 2018

https://www.sierraclub.org/sierra/you-can-t-hide-truth-without-action-global-warming-will-be-catastrophic

Baerbel W, Skeptical Science – updated 8 May 2016
https://skepticalscience.com/global-warming-scientific-consensus-basic.htm

Chapter 14 - Conception Deception

Jon Greenberg, Politifact - April 29, 2019

https://www.politifact.com/truth-o-meter/statements/2019/apr/29/donald-trump/donald-trump-repeats-falsely-doctors-mothers-decid/

Abby Vesoulis, Time – April 29, 2019

https://time.com/5579685/trump-late-term-abortion-false-claims

Sarah McCammon, NPR- January 17, 2017

https://www.npr.org/sections/thetwo-
way/2017/01/17/509734620/u-s-abortion-rate-falls-to-lowest-level-
since-roe-v-wade

Michell Ye Hee Lee, Washington Post – August 12, 2015

https://www.washingtonpost.com/news/fact-
checker/wp/2015/08/12/for-planned-parenthood-abortion-stats-3-
percent-and-94-percent-are-both-misleading/

Chapter 15 - Abstinence Makes The Hard Grow Longer

Carly Cassella, Science Alert – February 2, 2019

https://www.sciencealert.com/abstinence-only-education-is-more-
of-a-hindrance-than-a-help-in-the-us

Chapter 16 - Supremely Subjective

http://www.religioustolerance.org/scotuscon10.htm

Kai Sherwin, HuffPost – February 4, 2017

https://www.huffpost.com/entry/why-the-constitution-should-no-
longer-be-interpreted_b_58962bd2e4b0985224db55d1

Chapter 17- Mixed Up America

Rob Boston, Church & State Magazine - September 2018

https://www.au.org/church-state/september-2018-chuch-state-
magazine/featured/presecution-complex-religious-right

Jon Street, Campus Reform – November 5, 2018

https://www.campusreform.org/?ID=11482

https://www.edvisors.com/plan-for-college/money-saving-tips/colleges-with-free-tuition/countries-with-free-tuition/

Lisa Goetz, Investopedia - May 9, 2019

https://www.investopedia.com/articles/personal-finance/080616/6-countries-virtually-free-college-tuition.asp

https://www.thebalance.com/welfare-programs-definition-and-list-3305759

Lee Moran, HuffPost – April 16, 2016

https://www.huffpost.com/entry/bill-maher-church-tax-religion_n_5711dd19e4b0018f9cba30a7

Adam Lee, BigThink – January 22, 2012

Https://bigthink.com/daylight-atheism/why-we-should-tax-the-churches

Chapter 18 - Regulating Regulators

Hannah Waters, Audubon – January 17, 2017

https://www.audubon.org/news/why-we-need-strong-epa

David Roberts, Vox – March 28, 2017

https://www.vox.com/science-and-health/2017/3/2/14772518/environmental-regulations-jobs

Climate Change News – May 15 2015

https://www.climatechangenews.com/2018/05/15/ilo-green-economy-can-create-24-million-jobs-2030/

Jessica McDonald, FactCheck - November 9, 2018

https://www.factcheck.org/2018/11/clearing-up-the-facts-behind-trumps-clean-coal-catchphrase/

Brittany Patterson, Ohio Valley Resource, WFPL – February 4, 2019

https://wfpl.org/coal-comeback-coal-at-new-low-after-two-years-under-trump/

Chapter 19 - Going To Pot

Hannah Hartig and A.W. Geiger, Pew Research – October 10, 2018

https://www.pewresearch.org/fact-tank/2018/10/08/americans-support-marijuana-legalization/

Nicole Richter, Marijuana Break – July 16, 2019

https://www.marijuanabreak.com/going-to-prison-for-marijuana-possession

Chapter 20 - Foreign Frenzy

Marshall Zelinger, 9News - September 25, 2017

https://www.9news.com/article/news/local/verify/verify-can-nfl-players-get-fired-for-protesting-during-the-national-anthem/478614911

Vin Gupta, Vanessa Kerry, Foreign Policy - April 11, 2018

https://foreignpolicy.com/2018/04/11/foreign-aid-makes-america-safer/

https://www.countable.us/articles/9752-turn-u-s-ditch-foreign-aid

Chapter 21- Hypocritical Hypocrites

Jonathan Cohn, HuffPost – June 9, 2016

The Comprehensive Guide To Trump's Most Outrageous Statements

https://www.huffpost.com/entry/worst-trump-quotes_n_5756e8e6e4b07823f9514fb1?guccounter=1&guce_refe rrer=aHR0cHM6Ly93d3cuZ29vZ2xlLmNvbS8&guce_referrer_sig= AQAAANonVoXELvZOMfXwy68pjk7H35Frk0UDkDWewkV8sv50o gqL7O-gasBKavlKalJXoBru8AW0cqmDiz6fPLjPEq5ZPg2A7FDDdk91iA0 Eg5py1qe2ud2OCMNvvm2nvYcl6Vh2peQf4xpCX3DymOLDyUlV KPDn98iZFMsht54sd4KB

Ben Parker, Stephanie Steinbrecker and Kelsey Ronan, McSweeneys – November 5, 2018

https://www.mcsweeneys.net/articles/the-complete-listing-so-far-atrocities-1-546

Jeffrey Goldberg, The Atlantic

https://www.theatlantic.com/unthinkable/

Maegan Vazquez and Jim Acosta, CNN -August 20, 2019

https://www.keyt.com/news/politics/trump-outrages-leaders-by-saying-jews-disloyal-if-they-vote-for-dems/1111626297

John L. Micek, PennLive – August, 2017

https://www.pennlive.com/opinion/2017/08/these_are_the_15_wor st_things.html

Politifact – October, 2019

https://www.politifact.com/personalities/donald-trump/statements/byruling/pants-fire/

Chris Cillizza, CNN – December 20, 2018

https://www.cnn.com/2018/12/20/politics/trump-lines-of-the-year-the-point/index.html

Glenn Kessler, Salvador Rizzo and Meg Kelly, Washington Post – October 14, 2019

https://www.washingtonpost.com/politics/2019/10/14/president-trump-has-made-false-or-misleading-claims-over-days/?hpid=hp_ed-picks_fact-checker-1014%3Ahomepage%2Fstory-ans

Scott Neuman, NPR – May 2, 2018 (Chapter 21)

https://www.npr.org/sections/thetwo-way/2018/05/02/607638733/doctor-trump-dictated-letter-attesting-to-his-extraordinary-

David Hawkins, Quora – September, 2018 (Chapter 21)

https://www.quora.com/Donald-Trump-now-claims-article-two-of-the-constitution-gives-him-the-power-to-do-what-ever-he-wants-will-the-GOP-and-his-followers-support-this-idea/answer/David-Hawkins-96?ch=10&share=ff6d5624&srid=nKsJ

About the Authors

Samuel Warren Joseph:

His credits include the movie *Off Your Rocker*, a comedy-drama about a revolution in an old folks' home starring Milton Berle, Red Buttons, Dorothy Malone and Lou Jacobi. He has written animation episodes for such shows as *Duck Tales*, *Dennis the Menace*, *Batman: The Animated Series* and *Beast Wars*. In addition to his film and TV credits, Sam is a produced playwright. He wrote the book and co-wrote the songs for the stage musical, *Campaign*, which had its world premiere in 2010 at the Met Theatre in Los Angeles. In 2010, Sam's comedy about marital infidelity, *Two Times Two*, had its world premiere in New Orleans.

The film *Window of Opportunity*, which he wrote and directed, is based on his produced stage play of the same name. 2016 saw the world premiere of his play *Moral Imperative* about morality and murder in the world of academia. It also saw the workshop production of his new musical, *Psychosexual: A Love Story*. He is also the co-author, with Phil Proctor, of the play *God Help Us,* starring Ed Asner.

Phil Proctor:

Phil shared three Grammy nominations with **The Firesign Theatre** (whose archives were just purchased by The Library of Congress) and three daytime Emmys for voicing Howard DeVille on *Rugrats*, honored with a star on the Hollywood Walk of Fame. He has shared several Academy Awards for his voice work in the animé *Spirited Away* and numerous Disney/Pixar movies and most recently won an Audie for adding voices to the sci-fi epic *Battlefield Earth* and a Mark Time Award for *The Audio Adventure Book of Big Dan Frater*, created by Brian Howe. He has appeared in numerous interactive video games, most notably as the evil Dr. Vidic in **Assassin's Creed.**

Philip will be seen soon in a farcical (but true) horror film about you-know-who, and previously starred in Sam Joseph's comic political thriller, **Window of Opportunity,** produced by The Doors' John Densmore. He also co-starred in Henry Jaglom's first film, **A Safe Place** with Tuesday Wells, Orson Welles and Jack Nicholson and later in **Hollywood Dreams** and **Queen of the Lot**.

Other film credits include **The Adventures of Rocky and Bullwinkle**, **Amazon Women on the Moon**, **Lobsterman from Mars**, with the great Tony Curtis, and **Love Addict**, **The Selling** and **The Independent**, with his wife, Melinda Peterson. His television credits include **All in the Family, Night Court, the Golden Girls** and **Last Man Standing,** and he's a long time member of the renowned **Antaeus** theatre company in Glendale.

His autobiography, **Where's My Fortune Cookie?**, co-authored by Brad Schreiber, is also available as an enhanced audiobook read by the author, and **Americathon: The Skits behind the Script** and transcripts of the NPR comic series **Power,** both by Proctor & Bergman, are available at Bear Manor Media, while most of Firesign Theatre's classic albums and books can be found at www.firesigntheatre.com or through www.planetproctor.com.